3D Printing

CHERRY LAKE PUBLISHING • ANN ARBOR, MICHIGAN

by Terence O'Neill and Josh Williams

A Note to Adults: Please review the instructions for the activities in this book before allowing children to do them. Be sure to help them with any activities you do not think they can safely complete on their own.

A Note to Kids: Be sure to ask an adult for help with these activities when you need it. Always put your safety first!

Published in the United States of America by Cherry Lake Publishing
Ann Arbor, Michigan
www.cherrylakepublishing.com

Series Editor: Kristin Fontichiaro
Photo Credits: Cover and page 1, ©AP Images/dapd; page 4, ©ubrayj02/ www.flickr.com/CC-BY-2.0; pages 5, 7, 11, 17, 18, 29, ©makerbot/ www.flickr.com/CC-BY-2.0; page 9, ©Creative Tools/www.flickr.com/ CC-BY-2.0; page 13, ©dvanzuijlekom/www.flickr.com/CC-BY-SA-2.0; page 14, ©steveonjava/www.flickr.com/CC-BY-2.0; page 21, ©Tony Buser/www.flickr. com/CC-BY-SA-2.0; page 23, ©woodleywonderworks/www.flickr.com/ CC-BY-2.0; page 24, ©hackerfriendly/www.flickr.com/CC-BY-SA-2.0; page 25, ©See-ming Lee 李思明 SML/www.flickr.com/CC-BY-SA-2.0; page 28, ©Schmarty/www.flickr.com/CC-BY-2.0

Library of Congress Cataloging-in-Publication Data
O'Neill, Terence, 1984–
  3D printing/by Terence O'Neill and Josh Williams.
     pages cm.—(Makers as innovators) (Innovation library)
  Audience: Grade 4 to 6.
  Includes bibliographical references and index.
  ISBN 978-1-62431-138-3 (library binding)—ISBN 978-1-62431-270-0 (paperback)—ISBN 978-1-62431-204-5 (e-book)
  1. Three-dimensional printing—Juvenile literature. I. Williams, Josh, 1981– II. Title. III. Title: 3-D printing. IV. Title: Three-dimensional printing.
  TS171.8.O54 2013
  681'.62—dc23   2013004468

Cherry Lake Publishing would like to acknowledge the work of The Partnership for 21st Century Skills. Please visit www.p21.org for more information.

Printed in the United States of America
Corporate Graphics Inc.
July 2013
CLFA13

Contents

Chapter 1

What Is a 3D Printer?

Have you ever wanted to control how the things you use look, feel, and function? Imagine being able to think of a design for a hammer and then make that hammer right away. Maybe you want

3D printing could help you make simple parts to repair or improve your bicycle.

3D printers create items layer by layer.

to make a plastic hat for your dog. Or perhaps you need to replace a broken part on your bicycle. There is a type of machine that allows you to quickly create objects like this.

3D printers use designs made on computers to make three-dimensional objects right before your eyes. Three-dimensional objects are not flat like the words and images you print on paper. They are real-life objects that you can pick up and use! Users can control the size, shape, and even the material of their objects.

3D printing uses a process called additive layer manufacturing. During this process, a machine stacks layers of material to create objects. A 3D printer is kind of like a hot glue gun that puts out material in the shape that a computer describes.

At first, 3D printers were most useful to large companies that wanted to quickly make versions of new product ideas to use for testing. Today, many people are getting interested in this amazing technology.

A Very Short History of the 3D Printer

American inventor Charles Hull is largely credited with creating the idea of 3D printing. In 1986, he thought of using a **laser** to turn thin layers of liquid into a solid object. However, the technology available at the time made Hull's plan difficult. New lasers, computers, and materials had to be created before 3D printing became as useful as it is today.

The Internet has helped improve 3D printing by allowing people from all over the world to instantly share their knowledge. Also, small **microcontrollers** such as the Arduino are getting better and cheaper, making it easier to control motors and temperatures. This is very important for 3D printers.

Chapter 2

How People Are Using 3D Printers

Today, people are coming up with new and exciting uses for 3D printers all the time. Here are just a few examples of what these incredible machines can do.

Industrial Uses

The airplane company Airbus is trying to figure out a way to make a 3D printer that is as big as an airplane hangar. They are hoping to print entire airplanes

3D printers are becoming more and more popular.

with it! Companies have already been printing many types of tools. Some even print parts for race cars and motorcycles.

Medical and Health Uses

Because 3D printing can work with a wide variety of materials and the designs can be changed easily, health professionals are working with engineers to use it for medical applications. Strong, lightweight false teeth and replacement bones can be made with 3D printers. Even more complicated body parts, such as livers, ears, and skin, are also being tested.

What Does This Mean for Me?

3D printers are becoming faster, less expensive, and easier for everyday people to use. Libraries, schools, and **makerspaces** are buying 3D printers so people all around the world can make their own objects!

This allows individual people—not just giant airplane-making companies—to make and use new creations more quickly than they could otherwise.

Rings and other jewelry can be made with 3D printers.

And if you like the way something you've created looks and works, a 3D printer lets you create many more items just like it.

Everyday Uses

Artists at the small company Hot Pop Factory make jewelry designs based on mathematical formulas.

They use a 3D printer to manufacture their designs right away! They are able to print as many items as people order and ship them out the same day.

Sharing knowledge with other people is a big part of being a **maker**. Makers around the world contribute their 3D printer designs for others to use. One example is the personalized locks and keys that people are designing for themselves. These locks and keys are designed so that people can easily change them just a bit to make their own locking systems.

3D printers can even be used to make parts for creating more 3D printers. The RepRap project designs 3D printers that can reproduce themselves. This means that you can start with one 3D printer and make your own factory!

Makers love sharing. They like to learn about new things and get excited as they learn more. They also love to share what they've learned with others. The 3D printer company MakerBot encourages this kind of sharing. In addition to selling 3D printers, it runs a Web site that helps people share their 3D printer designs.

Thingiverse (*www.thingiverse.com*) allows users to create accounts and share their designs with other makers. Users can download one another's designs. They can print the items for themselves or change the designs to fit their personal needs. You don't have to own a MakerBot 3D printer to use these designs. You can use whatever 3D printer you have access to.

Since MakerBot Industries created Thingiverse in 2008, thousands of people have joined the site. By early 2013, more than 25,000 designs had been posted. That's more than 25,000 different designs you can look at, tweak, print, and ponder. Looking at designs created by other people is a great way to learn more about the 3D printing process.

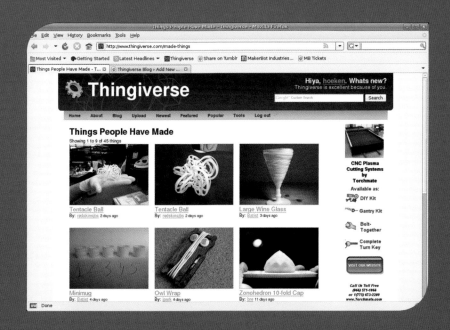

Chapter 3

3D Printing Now

Now we're going to walk through the steps that people all over the world follow to bring the designs they've thought of into reality. In this example, we're using the MakerBot Cupcake as our 3D printer. There are hundreds of other types of 3D printers. You can use any of them!

MakerBot is a company that makes 3D printers for makers, teachers, and other people who want to bring their ideas to life. These machines create objects from long pieces of plastic that look like giant strings of candy. This plastic bends to wrap around a spool. But it's as hard as a Lego piece when it comes out of the 3D printer.

This plastic is fed into the 3D printer. The printer melts the plastic and pushes it out through a part of the machine called an extruder. The extruder puts the melted plastic onto a metal plate. This is where the object will be formed. The extruder is moved around according to the design to draw a picture with the plastic. When that first picture is finished, the extruder begins putting another layer of plastic directly on top

A 3D printer's extruder draws designs using melted plastic.

of the first. It continues to add layers of plastic until the object is complete.

Reminder: This book is just an introduction! To print objects, read other sources and ask other experts!

The plastic for 3D printers is sold in spools and comes in many different colors.

To make 3D printed objects, you'll need several items:

- a 3D printer (such as the MakerBot Cupcake)
- plastic (usually sold in spools)
- a 3D design (an STL computer file)

- ReplicatorG (a **program** that slices the STL file into layers)

You can get an STL file a number of ways. You can borrow a friend's file, create one of your own, or download one from a Web site like Thingiverse.

Step 1: Search for a File on Thingiverse

Thingiverse has thousands of designs. Chances are good that they've got an object in their collection that is right for you. But how do you find it? First, think about what you want to make. Do you want something useful, like a set of pliers? Maybe you'd rather make an awesome model of a dragon. Thingiverse might have what you're looking for. Giving some thought to what you want to make before you begin searching can help make the search more effective.

Once you've got a good idea, enter it in the search box in the top right corner of the Web page. The Thingiverse search tries to match the words you've entered to the object's description. So typing just a couple of words usually works better than typing a whole sentence. "Pliers" will work better than "hold stuff together." "Dragon" will work much better than "fire-breathing lizard with wings."

You might not find anything in your search. Luckily, Thingiverse provides other options for finding cool designs. The Browse button near the top of the page is especially useful. You can use it to look for cool designs grouped into categories like "Fashion" or "Gadgets." You can also look for designs under the Things drop-down menu.

Once you've picked a design, you need to move the design onto your computer so that you can get it ready to print. To download the file, simply click on its title along the left side of the Web page.

Step 2: Slice the File Using ReplicatorG

The 3D designs you download from Thingiverse come as STL files. In this example, we use a program called ReplicatorG to slice the 3D design in the STL file into layers. The layers are so thin that each one is almost flat. As the layers are stacked on top of each other, they begin to form an object. Each layer might be different from the last. The top layers might look very different from the bottom layers.

To continue with the example, you'll need to download ReplicatorG onto your computer. To download it, go to *http://replicat.org/download*.

A Few Words on Safety

3D printers are completely safe if you handle them properly. But you need to be careful. Here are a few areas to pay specific attention to:

- Parts of 3D printers get hot enough to melt plastic. This means they are also hot enough to melt you. Give the machine space while it is working.
- Once printing has started, do not touch the platform, the extruder, or any of the interior parts of the 3D printer. If you must adjust anything, unplug the machine and wait until it has cooled off.
- Use 3D printers in a space where there is plenty of fresh air. Keep a fan running nearby or open a window to help move the air around.

Next, run the ReplicatorG program. Then open the STL file that you've downloaded to print. Click on Generate GCode to get ReplicatorG started on slicing your design into layers.

Once ReplicatorG has finished slicing your file, you are ready to print out your project. There are two ways to get your file to the printer. You can either connect your computer directly or use an SD card. An SD card is a small card that can be plugged into

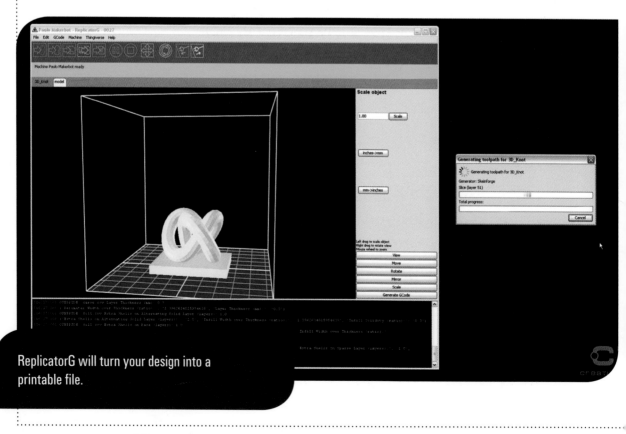

ReplicatorG will turn your design into a printable file.

various devices and used to store computer files. Either way, you're very close to putting down some plastic.

This is only a brief introduction to get you going. It often takes time to get 3D printers to work correctly. The directions are often very detailed. We're just introducing the main ideas here.

Step 3: Print Your Object

There are many different companies that make 3D printers, so there are many different kinds of 3D printers. All of them get ready to print in their own way. They must heat up, get the extruder into the right position, and follow other steps. But all of them require being connected. Make sure your 3D printer is plugged into the wall and that the computer or SD card with the GCode is properly connected.

Your 3D printer will soon begin oozing out your object. It might be designed to put down a "raft." This is a base layer of plastic that your object will sit on. This is just so the print will go more smoothly. Even so, you'll need to pay attention to your print. Why? Because it's cool to watch! You can also notice things that might go wrong, stop the print, and safely correct the mistake before trying again.

Give your object at least five minutes to cool down after it finishes printing. Then it is ready to be taken out, snapped off its raft, and used. You can use sandpaper to sand your object's edges down and make them smoother. If you've gotten this far, give yourself a huge round of applause. You've printed your first object!

Remember that all of these pieces—the 3D printer, Thingiverse designs, ReplicatorG—are made possible by people sharing ideas with one another. This technology becomes more widespread as members of the 3D printing community share their knowledge. They do this by creating and using **open source** computer files and by sitting together around a table, talking and eating lunch. Now you are a member of this community!

Chapter 4

Designing Your Own Object

Y ou might not always find the 3D printer designs you are looking for online. In that case, you might want to create your own designs. There

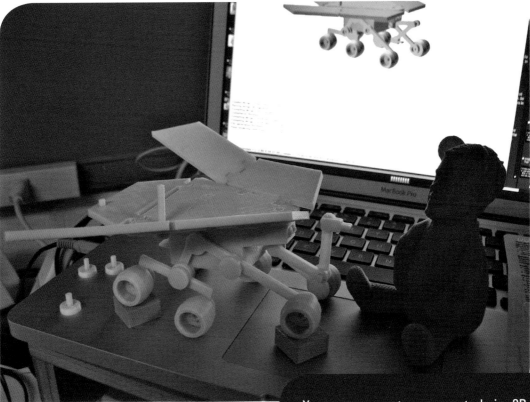

You can use computer programs to design 3D models of almost anything you can imagine.

are a variety of 3D modeling programs you can use to design your own object. We'll briefly discuss three of them. All three are free and available to download or use online!

Trimble SketchUp
www.sketchup.com
This is one of the easiest modeling programs to use. There are helpful tutorials, and it connects to the Google 3D Warehouse, where you can find and share

Magic Arms

As 3D printing technology improves, it is being used to improve people's lives. A young girl named Emma Lavelle was born with a condition that makes it difficult for her to use her arms. A device known as the Wilmington Robotic Exoskeleton (WREX) allows people with this condition to move their arms. However, when Emma was two years old, the WREX weighed nearly as much as she did. Doctors used 3D printers to create a special version of WREX that was light and small enough for Emma to use. Now Emma can use her arms, and 3D printing will make it easy to modify her WREX as she grows up.

3D models. This allows you to use other people's designs as a base for your own ideas.

123D Catch

www.123dapp.com

This collection of programs includes an iPad app that converts photos into printable files. Another feature

If you are using a school computer, ask permission before downloading any programs.

The 123D Catch app offers an easy way to turn photos into 3D models.

allows you to sculpt your own models. It also includes a 3D design studio that exists entirely online. It's all free, too!

Blender

www.blender.org

This free 3D modeling program is available for download for both Windows and Mac computers. It is more advanced than Trimble SketchUp or 123D Catch. It also takes longer to use.

Blender is more difficult to learn than some other 3D programs, but it offers more options for advanced users.

Chapter 5

Where Can I Find 3D Printers?

You probably don't have your own 3D printer. Luckily, there are many places that offer 3D printers for people to use. Here are a few places where you might find one:

1. Makerspaces

A great place to look for 3D printers is your local makerspace. Makerspaces usually have some of the coolest technology around. They can also help you meet people who are excited about this technology. Makerspaces form to allow people with different interests and skills to meet and work on different projects in the same space. One maker might build a desk while another writes the code for a video game.

Makerspaces often allow individuals, clubs, and businesses to share the use of 3D printers. The people at these places are always happy to have kids and other interested people just pop in for a hello or a 3D printing session.

2. Libraries

Public libraries are starting to catch on to how useful and easy 3D printing is. Many are beginning to partner with local organizations like makerspaces. Some are even buying their own 3D printers.

3. Shapeways

The company Shapeways created a way to print people's designs for them. They use high quality materials such as different types of metal. At the Shapeways Web site (*www.shapeways.com*), you can purchase thousands of different products designed by everyday people and created using 3D printers. You can also work with professional designers to create your own products. You can even sell your designs for people to use.

4. Manufacturing

Many companies and universities use 3D printers to build models and test ideas. These places are often available for public tours. The people who work there are happy to answer questions. If you find a local company that uses 3D printing, get in contact with them and see if they would like to host a group of you and your friends.

A Member of the Movement

Now that you have read this book, you've learned what 3D printers are, what they're capable of, and how you can print your own customized objects. Now you know a bit about one of the most exciting technologies around!

3D printing is becoming better, more popular, and more important. Now that you've got the basics down, you can start building your own tools and toys. Go out and become part of the movement! Design, print, build, and share your knowledge.

What will you create with a 3D printer?

What if you don't have any of these resources near you? You can buy your own 3D printer. Unfortunately, these machines aren't cheap. Form a group with your friends and raise money. You can also talk to your teachers and librarians to see if they can find a way for you to try this technology.

Glossary

laser (LAY-zur) a device that emits a very narrow, intense beam of light; lasers have uses ranging from surgery to welding to reading CDs

maker (MAY-kur) a person who invents, creates, or fabricates something

makerspaces (MAY-kur-spay-suz) places where makers come together to make, tinker, invent, and share

microcontrollers (MYE-kro-kuhn-trohl-urz) small computers capable of carrying out simple programs

open source (OH-puhn SOURS) freely available and allowed to be changed by anyone

program (PROH-gram) a series of instructions, written in a computer language, that controls the way a computer works

Find Out More

BOOKS

Prusa, Josef. *Getting Started with RepRap: 3D Printing on Your Desktop*. Sebastopol, CA: O'Reilly Media/Make, 2013.

Make: Ultimate Guide to 3D Printing. Sebastopol, CA: O'Reilly Media/Make, 2012.

WEB SITES

ReplicatorG
http://replicat.org
Download the computer program you need to slice up 3D models into printable designs.

RepRap
http://reprap.org
Learn more about the project to create a 3D printer that can build copies of itself.

Shapeways
www.shapeways.com
Search among thousands of 3D printed objects created by makers around the world.

Thingiverse
www.thingiverse.com
Search for designs to print on a 3D printer and share your own creations.

Index

About the Authors

Terence O'Neill (left) works in libraries in Ann Arbor, Michigan. He loves all kinds of libraries, learning about new things, and connecting people with learning.

Josh Williams (right) is the shop manager at All Hands Active, a makerspace in Ann Arbor, Michigan. When he's not organizing workers and volunteers or teaching classes on programming, Arduinos, and 3D printers, he spends time hiking with his wife.